A family portrait, circa 1936

My grandparents, Ivar and Edna Tilghman Larson,
with son Hilary (my dad)

AMANDA LARSON

Healing from a Grandmother's Heart

Wisdom and Power to Heal Your Life

THE LARSON INSTITUTE

WASHINGTON, D.C.

Library of Congress Number: 00-190629

ISBN: 0-9679575-0-8

Book design and cover art by Stephen Kraft
Printed by McBride's Printing & Graphics, Inc., Gaithersburg, MD

First Edition
Published in 2000 by The Larson Institute.

This book may be purchased in quantity at a discount for educational or promotional use. Please contact: Special Markets, The Larson Institute, PO Box 21241, Washington, DC 20009.

To all who knew
Edna Tilghman Larson,
and all who will
know her through
this book

Table of Contents

Acknowledgments

First and foremost, I would like to thank Michael Kane for his tremendous support and superior editing skills. Without him, this book might not have made it into your hands today.

For standing by me and supporting my vision when others didn't quite see the world as I did, I wish to thank Christiana Carty, Lord Carrett, and Michael Gilles. Thank you, Diane Ney, for being a good friend with a sharp eye for detail, and thanks to Mary, Larry and Nick at McBride's Printing for their good words and fine work. And Stephen Kraft, you designed a beautiful book.

A big thank you to Chris McDonald at keybridge.net for being the best.

I would like to express my deep appreciation to the following people for their contribution to this book—the gifts of wisdom, light, and just plain good advice: Trudy Fenton, Phyllis Burlage, Bill Tilghman, Phyllis Blaunstein, Margo Baldwin, Steve Evans, Paul Dankanich, Bonnie Bates, Judy Eggleston, Richard Hewlett, Irene Hishmeh, George Fassiadis, Durelle Jones, Lynne Glassman, Diane Pelavin, Ann Miller, Kim Perino, Sherry Schiller.

I love you, Mom and Dad.

Know Yourself
Trust Yourself
Be Yourself

Then You Will Know How to Live

The Creator's Great Truth

The Creator of the Universe sat by himself and pondered his dilemma. He had the secret to a happy life, one that he dearly wanted to share with all of humankind, but sadly, he could see that they were not ready. This great truth is *everyone can create their own reality.* He had to hide this truth until all of the people were ready to listen and truly believe. But where?

He consulted the Stars of the Sky. "We'll ride the truth along the Milky Way, and take it to space," they said. "No," said the Creator, ' they will go there and find it."

He asked Old Mother Four Winds. "I'll blow the truth to the top of the Earth," she said. "No," said the Creator, "they will go there, too, and will find it too soon."

He spoke to the ancient master of the seas, the Giant Whale. "I shall take it to the very bottom of the sea. No one will find it there!" he said. "Ah, but they will go to the bottom of the sea sooner than you think," said the Creator. "They must find this truth at precisely the right time."

Despairing, he called to the Snake, the high master of wisdom. "What shall I do?" the Creator cried. The Wise Snake looked at him kindly, and said "Cloak it in intuition, and put it inside their hearts. They will only look there when they are ready to hear."

The Creator said, "And so it shall be."

Time went on, and proved the Snake to be correct. As the new millenium approached, the Creator saw that the time for Truth had arrived. Boldly, human beings the world over started discovering the secret of life—that happiness is a birthright, and that we create it through love. These brave beings set forth to spread the word that heaven was within our grasp, right here on Earth. All transpired just as it was supposed to.

The Creator smiled.

Inspired by Native American Legend

Introduction

*E*dna Tilghman Larson, my grandmother, was a very special person. Born in 1908, she grew up on an historic farm in southern New Jersey that was once owned by a relative of Benjamin Franklin. Edna's own ancestor had served as General George Washington's aide-de-camp during the Revolutionary War. While Edna's personal background connected her to the origins of our nation in significant ways, her spiritual roots were even more deeply grounded within the earth itself. Her mother, Hilda, was a wise and visionary healer who passed her knowledge and wisdom on to her daughter. Hilda taught Edna to make and use herbal and flower remedies, and started her on a lifelong spiritual path that brought healing and love to everyone who ever came within her circle of family and friendship.

The story of wise and magical women in our family goes back a long, long way. When I was an adult, many years after Edna had passed away, I asked my father about the family's healers. All he knew was what Edna had told him—that the daughters had been taught the magic of the world and were well-known as healers of body and soul. I know from Edna's personal papers that treasured recipes and information were passed down through the centuries, sometimes on paper but mostly by practical instruction. There is a thread that ties all of the daughters, and one day I hope to know who the founding matriarch of this family might have been. For now, I know the joy of the light energy that swirls within and around me, and I thank Edna for the gifts of spirit and earth she so beautifully passed on to me.

Edna was taught the magic of healing in a unique place. Sharon Plantation, the Tilghman family farm, was a lovely 240-acre pre-Revolutionary bit of history—it had farmland, woods, meadows, and best of all, a clear stream called Barker's Brook running swiftly through the center of it. There was also an enchanted home that was built in the 1740s. The Sharon of my grandmother's and great-grandmother's day no longer exists except in my memory and a few photographs. It lives on, however, in the power of the herbal healing remedies that the women in my family made and used, as well as in the healing practice that I continue today.

Edna's warmth and wisdom became the guiding forces in my life. She believed in the Golden Rule—you remember, "Do unto others as you would have them do unto you." She was loving, straightforward, and magical. She also was practical, no-nonsense, and very funny. The roots of the woman I am today are wound securely in her spirit, and through her influence I am able to continue the healing presence that was begun so long ago.

This book is a tribute to my grandmother, Edna Tilghman Larson. As you read it, I hope you get to know this warm, funny woman and see how her practical approach to life makes so much sense. Her ability to mix the spiritual, practical, and magical sides of life is one that I've tried to emulate. My life can be summed up in one word—joyful. I learned how to be that way from her. I'm thankful every single day.

This book, *Healing From A Grandmother's Heart*, is an amalgam of wisdom, sayings, recipes, and ideas that flowed from Edna to me. I have arranged it so that in the beginning, you'll meet and get to know her a bit. She had very definite feelings about why some people heal and others don't, and I begin with that. The Catalyst Steps, my name for Edna's rules of living, are presented in the next six chapters. In the balance of the book, you'll learn even more about her, and by reading these final chapters you'll have the inspiration to make your life seem newer, more loving and ultimately all that you want it to be. Finally, I've included some of her charming and unique recipes—for Violet syrup, Horehound-Catnip drops, and other such old-fashioned, but effective, remedies.

Edna has had a profound impact on my life, and I sincerely hope she will do the same with yours.

This book will share with you all that made Edna special. I hope you'll be inspired by her words and by her example. Stories from and about her as well as quotes from her will be highlighted in the chapters to come. Her life was not one of fame or riches, yet we would all be incredibly wealthy if we lived our lives according to her principles.

It's my hope that you'll see the depth and beauty of the tapestry of life she wove with her wisdom and healing ability. She knew what wise ones have known throughout the ages—that we have the ability to make our own reality. I hope she inspires you to make your life all that it should be.

Everyone's work shall become manifest abundantly

THE BOOK OF I CORINTHIANS

1

A Little Bit about Edna

As a young girl, Edna often drove a truck loaded *with tomatoes from her family farm in Jobstown, New Jersey, to the Campbells Soup Company in Camden. Her sister-in-law, my Aunt Pete, told me how she would drive all the way to Camden and never drop one tomato from that truck. The particular vehicle she used was an old-fashioned flatbed that had to be loaded just right or all the tomatoes would end up in the street. This was in the late 1920s, too, with bumpy back roads—no interstate! Most girls would have hated the job, but not Edna. Why?*

"I was on the road with the wind in my hair. I felt free. Besides, I was much better at it than my brothers!"

Edna was a unique individual and the most important influence on my life. She was a gregarious woman who loved people but also kept to herself. My grandmother was the glue of the family, always making sure we all kept in touch even though some of us lived far away. She needed her "Mama Nature time," her quiet time outside, and would allow nothing but an emergency to disturb it. She was honored to be a healer, but never boasted about her power or that of her mother, from whom she inherited the gift. Edna loved deeply, but was not always able to show it. She adored animals, too much actually, because after her beloved collie died she could not bring herself to get another dog. "Too painful to lose them," she said.

Edna was an educated woman living with a husband who did not encourage her ambitions. She managed to get her Bachelor's degree by squeezing it in between her various jobs on the family farm. She would tell me of running down the long lane that led from the farm to the railroad tracks to flag down the train that would take her to Rider College, in Trenton. She was never able to convince my grandfather of the value of advanced education—she would have loved to have been a doctor. Remember, this was an age when men ruled the roost, and as gifted as Edna was, she came from a traditional family. Grandad may not have been keen on her going to medical school, but he did give her a precious gift—freedom. "I would have died if Ivar kept me under his thumb," she said to my mother. "Literally. I need to follow my spirit."

I've come to realize over the years that Edna was honored to have healing gifts and great wisdom—although she did not think she was particularly special. Her mother, Hilda Loveless Tilghman, was her inspiration and teacher, and the energetic healing principles that Hilda passed down were so much a part of life that they were just...there. Edna's way of teaching was the same as Hilda's. She started when I could barely walk and talk and made it a part of my everyday experience, just like her mother had done for her.

*"There are elements of magic in everyday living—
it's not so hard to see it. People are trained these days to
see with only their eyes. To truly see, you must use your
eyes, mind, spirit, and soul. Then magic appears in every corner!"*

Edna's experience in this world began on a cold day in Feb-
ruary, 1908. She was the only daughter in a brood of four that
also included Charlie, Malcolm, and baby Walter who died very,
very young. The family farm, as I've said, was originally chris-
tened Sharon Plantation. The original farmhouse reputedly dated
back to the late seventeenth century, but the house my grandmother grew up in was built in the decades just prior to the
American Revolution. The house was historic, beautiful, and
quite large. When the Tilghman family moved in, they renamed
the property. It became Pine Lane Farm, in honor of the lovely
pine trees that graced the lane leading up from the main road.

Growing up as a Tilghman meant knowing that your colorful family was a part of history. Our family tree includes Tench
Tilghman, who served as General George Washington's trusted
aide-de-camp during the American Revolution. There was also
our cousin Bill Tilghman, deputy to Bat Masterson in Dodge
City and the man who captured the infamous outlaw Bill Doolin.

And what about Edna's family on her mother's side? The
Loveless family may not be as colorful, but here is where the
wisdom, grace, and healing power come from. According to my
grandmother, this talent for healing has been passed down

8

through the women in the family. Of course, since discretion beats the stake any day, that talent had to be hidden occasionally during those times in history when wise women herbalists were considered witches. Truth always wins in the end, however, so the secrets that were whispered to daughter upon daughter survive and flourish today, and of that I am exceedingly grateful.

Edna's youth and young adulthood were spent at Pine Lane Farm. She lived in a place that included meadows, cropland, woods, Barker's Brook, and every plant and flower that was known to Burlington County. When it was time to go to college or go to Philadelphia to shop, there was the train that came by at the end of the lane.

> *I remember watching the TV show "Petticoat Junction" with Edna one evening. "That was just like life at the farm!" she said. "We could run down the lane and flag down the conductor, and he would stop for us. When I was going to college he would blow the whistle to make sure I got down there on time."*

My grandmother's youth was average in many ways. In an agricultural family, there are jobs that have to be done, and that's that. In between the regular chores that were involved in running the farm, Edna's mother would take her outside and teach her about the healing plants. When it came time to make medicines, Edna was there at her side. The tinctures and poultices that they used have proven startlingly effective for me, and I swear sometimes I can hear Hilda (Edna's mom, my great-grand-mother) chuckling at me somewhere in the distance, wondering why I would ever doubt.

One particular healing modality that Edna used frequently was something called "taking the flowers." It was the one thing I never made with Edna, and had no idea how she made them. I just knew that each flower was for a specific "fit," as she would call it. If I was upset about something, I would have it in my water or milk. She never said much about it, it was just one of her many medicines, and I remember her telling me that she had learned to make them from her mother.

Years later I was introduced to Bach Flower Essences by a friend. It seemed similar, but this was back in the days when I was ignoring my life plan and trying to make it as an actress. I had put all of Edna's papers away and hadn't looked at them for a long, long time. After using the Essences, a bell went off in my head and I went racing to the box where I kept her papers. Sure enough, there were the explanations, but no instructions! I eventually apprenticed with a dear and talented herbalist in California who showed me how to make them. Healers like my grandmother and great-grandmother have been using Essences for generations and generations—they just called them by a different name.

Edna grew up and married my grandfather, Ivar, when she was in her mid-twenties. They had only one child, my father, Hilary. I know she was concerned that the line of healing would end with her. (My Aunt Pete, her sister-in-law, told me so.) She contented herself with her own knowledge and skills, and set about discovering all the plants and wonders on the property of the home she and my Grandad bought in Florence, New Jersey.

Then Hilary and my mother married. A year and a half later, I arrived. There is a photo of my great-grandmother Hilda holding me as a tiny baby. She died shortly thereafter. Edna was convinced that her mother stayed on to make sure the line would not be broken. When Hilda was assured that it would go on, she was free to go on to her next adventure (something else my Aunt Pete told me!).

Edna's world was one of peace. She knew that her circle would be unbroken. Tremendous faith was one of her hallmarks. My grandmother's only major concern was time. She gave me a tremendous amount of information, and left recipes and messages for me to use but she wanted more time with me. I found a letter years later, after my dad had passed away, that was sent from Edna to my mother. Edna and Grandad had moved to Tempe, Arizona, in 1967. They had been there less than a year, and were ready to move back to New Jersey. My parents and I had moved into the house in Florence after their departure. The property was large almost four acres, and the plan was for my grandparents to build a small home on the grounds so we could all be near each other again. The joys of Arizona were no match for the joys of family.

That was the plan. Then, just after Edna's sixtieth birthday, she passed away in her sleep in Tempe. The house Edna planned on was never built—in fact, my little family fragmented and the togetherness she sought was now impossible to have. I spun away, far away from the gifts I had been given. I had my own spiritual work to do, and through it I have found my way back to my original joy. It took years to rediscover, but I am here to make the most of the divine work of the women in my family.

I've given you a short history of Edna, and now I'd like to tell you about her wisdom and healing abilities. She always said that healing came in many different forms. It wasn't just a matter of treating a terrible case of poison ivy or easing a ferocious headache. Edna felt that true healing began in the mind and soul. She felt that if she could calm a person's mind, encourage lightness of heart, and impart a sense of peace and order in the universe, she had done her job well. Life to her was a tremendous learning experience, and the way to learn effectively was to look at your circumstances with new eyes. See the pleasures, see the lessons, and use your will to make positive changes. A good attitude and a willingness to look deeply for answers were the ingredients to a successful life.

> *Taken from a letter Edna wrote to her son, my father, when he was in the Naval Reserve:*
> *"…The truth will tease you. You'll think it's outside you, and you'll see it waving at you from down the lane, very pretty and bright. You'll be tempted to dance, but remember, it's an illusion, a decoy meant to keep you from your heart's desire. Go inside, to your heart, and that's where you'll find your truth. Pull away the veils of*

blame, guilt, and pride, and there it is."

Edna taught me that a fulfilling life is available to anyone who truly desires it. Achieving fulfillment requires mastery of self, however, and that can be a tall order. My dear grandmother knew the secret of the ages, which is this: we all have the ability to create our own reality. The issues of life are not always as they appear. Illusion surrounds us. When we pierce that curtain of illusion and learn how to live life on our own terms, circumstances can change dramatically. We must consistently expect the best, no matter what the outward appearances. Edna learned how to do this. She began teaching me, and I have since found many other teachers who have imprinted my life with a sense of wonder and expectation.

As Edna's granddaughter, I have a legacy of healing. However, there is a crucial difference between me and my ancestors—I have no children. The line ends here. I have been given a choice between living my life and taking this knowledge with me when I'm through or leaving it for an entire world to use and benefit from. I choose the latter. Writing this book is my way to share my grandmother's wisdom.

This book is Edna's gift to you, through me. The circle will remain unbroken.

All things are possible to those who believe

2

The Catalyst Steps

"*Step by step, year by year, life should become richer and sweeter. If it isn't, change your recipe for living.*"

Edna was a woman who lived an ordinary life in an extraordinary way. She was able to see through the veils that sometimes cloud our vision. It's the kind of life we'd all like to live.

Life is a series of daily "stuff" punctuated with some highs and lows. We've been conditioned to look at the activities that take up most of our days as filler, things to do while we're waiting for the big things to come along. Looking at daily occurrences in a new way, however, can become the basis for extraordinary living.

Edna could take a regular, average day and turn it into a fairy tale if she chose to. Even if she never left the house, never took a call, never spoke to anyone other than the milkman and the postman—she could have the most fabulous adventures.

My grandmother decided when she was a young woman that she would live by her own set of rules no matter what others said. Those rules were based on her theory that life is overwhelmingly good. She had the good fortune to learn that the experience of life comes directly from your attitude about it.

Instead of looking for difficulty, she cultivated joy. The most average of days still contains many delights and pleasures. For Edna, she might see a butterfly land on the windowsill, two doves making mournful cries from their perch outside the window, and squirrels dashing about doing whatever it is squirrels do. She would smell the bread baking, enjoy her second cup of coffee, and read the latest letter from her niece, Mary. She would hear the crunch of gravel on the driveway, telling her that my grandfather was home from work. She could hear the gentle, comforting rumble of the trains that ran not too far away from her house. All this in an average day. What made it special? Attitude.

Edna appreciated her world. She had a choice of being blind to the small delights of daily living, or embracing them. Because of this lovely way of life expression, people were drawn to her. She had a knack for being happy. No small thing, as most of us are constantly searching for that elusive happiness!

Edna's magic was contained in the way she combined her philosophy of life with natural gifts of the earth to support herself emotionally in positive ways. She didn't have to take a flower cure or herbal remedy, though she did frequently. All she had to do was go outside in the spring and inhale the fragrance of her lilac bushes.

My grandmother was a model for me. She was able to see into a person's heart, and it was a skill she developed to an amazing degree. Along with her sense of deep knowing, she also understood what was real and important in this life. She could spot a phony at twenty paces, had no use for shallow relationships, and would only fib to avoid hurting someone else's feelings.

Edna felt that the Eleventh Commandment should have been "Thou shalt not hurt someone's feelings if you can help it."

Edna always did her best to be kind to others, and to be kind to herself as well. As a healer, she knew that it was imperative to remain centered and positive so that she could be of maximum benefit to those who came to her for help. She had guidelines for her life, and was convinced that following them was the answer to keeping her mind clear of negativity. I call these guidelines the Catalyst Steps.

"You can't have a good day if it's filled with stinky thoughts."

I love her use of the term "stinky thoughts." It's a great image. It brings home just how those old thoughts can grab hold and smell up the place, getting in the way of your good! Here are Edna's Catalyst Steps:

- Get rid of—completely destroy—any negative images of yourself. This means all those old tapes in your head that say "I'm fat" or "I'm stupid" or "I'm a failure."
- Starting this minute, look at life in the affirmative.

- Begin watching your language for negatives. Someone once said that man (or woman) should use words only to bless, heal, and uplift. There is no quicker way to start the happiness flowing in your life.

- Forgive and release the need to blame. Not only others— you must forgive and cast blame aside for yourself as well.

- Start loving and quit hating.

Think of these steps as a catalyst to a more satisfied life. Just as you prepare a canvas before you begin painting, you must prepare your mind by cleaning out the collection of dismal thoughts that may have collected over the years. Let sunshine into those dark corners! Once positive thinking starts streaming into your mind and daily life, you'll find it much easier to create a new world for yourself.

We must prepare ourselves to accept our good. We must find belief in our true nature, that of love. By following the Catalyst Steps, we will come to a place of balance that will ultimately lead to a fuller expression of life on earth. In the next five chapters these steps are reviewed.

Be wise, and make my heart glad

THE BOOK OF PROVERBS

3

Goodbye to the Failure Script

*M*e: *"Mom-Mom, I want to be queen."*
   Edna: "OK, you can be anything you want."
   Me: "So I'm queen now?"
   Edna: "You are exactly what you think you are. Just remember that Mommy is the queen mother, so she is in charge and knows what's best."
   Me: "OK."

   Then she made me a crown.
   (This story was relayed by my Dad, twenty years later.)

The first Catalyst Step is one that may take some time to accomplish. The reason is that many of us are programmed with some startling negativity and have been since childhood. These unpleasant thoughts have become such a part of our lives that we're not even aware of them, yet they exist, day after day, keeping us from accomplishing our heart's desire.

Were you told as a child that you were fat or dumb? Have you been told over and over again that you can't advance in your job because you don't have a college education? Have you been carrying tons of guilt because your parents said you weren't good enough? These are all examples of negative programming. We heard it enough, and now we believe it. Perhaps we attempt to lose weight, advance in our jobs, or leave our hometown. Our attempt to take a giant step forward doesn't pan out and we end up back at square one thus reinforcing the negative. We keep reading self-help books, and find they don't get us anywhere. Life becomes more of an existence than a joy. We accept the situation resignedly, and just live out our lives.

Edna gave me the key to making my life a happy one, not just an existence. Belief in myself was the only thing that made a difference. Achieving that belief is a process that begins with deprogramming.

Take some time. Pull out a pencil and paper. Think about your childhood, and the way you felt then. Remember the reasons why you felt you couldn't measure up, the unpleasant things that were said about you, and the terrible things you thought about yourself. Write them down. Take your time and go into as much detail as you wish. Example: Up until I was about ten or so, I sang my little heart out all the time. Then I tried out for our church choir. I wasn't accepted, and I overheard the choirmaster telling my mother that I couldn't sing. Well, he should know, right? I barely opened my mouth to sing even "Happy Birthday" from that day forward. When I had to sing in mandatory music class in seventh grade, I lip-synched. I was completely embarrassed and decided never to let anyone hear my singing ever again.

Finally, when I was thirty-five, I decided to take a voice

class. I had seen an advertisement for one of those voice classes for "people who can't sing." I had always wanted to sing, even though I could barely croak out a lullaby, so I figured I had nothing to lose. Here I was, in a group class with others who also felt they couldn't carry a tune, so I wasn't embarrassed. Guess what? I could sing. I ended up taking some private lessons and even sang a little on stage. All those years I had a failure script and it turned out to be completely untrue. My mind and my fear kept me from doing something wonderful and fun.

You must believe in yourself, and believe in your ability to create your own reality. You may have the most amazing talent hidden away just waiting for your mind to release it.

Edna always told me to "think it and be it." I didn't understand that until I was an adult. As you think so shall you be.

As of this moment, I expect every one of you to smash and destroy every unpleasant, untrue thing that's ever been said about you. Then I want you to do the same thing with every unpleasant, untrue thing you've ever said about yourself. Do this with intention.

Now I want you to visualize these untruths recorded on a big, outdated eight-track tape. Just one big continuous loop of junk. Make sure it's all on there.

Now smash it to bits.

This is without a doubt the most important thing you can

do to initiate or intensify any healing, whether the healing is emotional, physical, or spiritual. All of that negativity and hurt need to be hauled out, gotten rid of, and kept out. Make a mental note to smash that eight-track tape every time you feel yourself about to say "I'm so fat" or "I'm unlovable" or "I'm stupid."

Visuals are a great help in deprogramming. Giving certain kinds of thoughts a physical aspect makes it easier to section them off, and get rid of them. Smashing something solid—even if it's just in your mind—can make a very large impact on the subconscious.

Remember to smash that tape to bits in your mind the minute you feel an old limitation coming upon you. You'll not only get rid of the thought, you'll start laughing to yourself because you're smashing an eight-track tape in your head! It all comes down to replacing a bad thought with a good one. When you smile, the world looks brighter, and you can easily replace the failure thought with a new, beneficial one. Instead of "I'm stupid," start playing a new tune, one that says "I'm very bright." Instead of "I'll never get anywhere," try "I'm on my way to the top of my profession." This is the first, essential step in breaking your old patterns and getting yourself set up for a better life.

Make an agreement that you will start today to treat yourself with the love and respect you deserve. Start by going easy on yourself. None of us are perfect, though heaven knows we sometimes think that we should be. When we treat those around us with love and good intentions, we are being the best we can be. Always affirm your essential goodness.

Our surroundings have tremendous impact on us. You've got to take good care of yourself and associate with people who share your positive way of thinking. If you find that your friends are constantly feeding you unpleasant remarks, find new buddies. If your mother criticizes you constantly, tell her—nicely, of course—to cut it out. You need to create a support network for yourself, and you want to be surrounded with as much good "stuff" as possible.

Your health and well-being depend on loving yourself as completely as you can.

Mom-Mom and I spotted a light blue chrysalis hanging from a branch on the maple tree behind the kitchen.

Me: "Are you sure a butterfly will come out of there?"
Edna: "Absolutely."
Me: "How do you know?"
Edna: "The caterpillar knows that her destiny is to be a butterfly. She believes it and she becomes it."
Me: "Just like that?"
Edna: "Just like that."

The meditation of my heart shall be of understanding

THE BOOK OF PSALMS

4

Life in the Affirmative

I make it a practice to use and enjoy all of my lovely things. Good jewelry, fine crystal, fancy china, whatever—I use it and get tremendous pleasure out of it. Edna never put things away for special occasions. "Every day has the potential to be special," she would say. Edna felt that as the caretaker of pretty things she had a responsibility to use them. "Anything that is beautiful or elegant must be used—it goes against God to keep beauty hidden!"

My mother, at a holiday dinner when I was a tot: "Edna! Don't let her carry that crystal! What if it breaks?"

Edna: "To everything there is a season. Here, honey, now carry this one."

This is a favorite story of mine because it's about complete trust—not just trust in my ability to carry the glass, but trust in the Universe to make everything OK. If it's time for the glass to go to that great glass shop in the sky, then it'll happen, and, well, there's nothing to be done. As Edna always said, "If it's not breathing, it's replaceable."

Life in the Affirmative

Living life in the affirmative is the second Catalyst Step. It starts inside. Waking up every morning with a sweet smile on your face is the best and only way to start the day. Starting tomorrow morning, be aware of the way in which you face the day. Do you scramble out of bed, mutter your way to the shower, down some coffee, and blast out the door?

Start your morning ritual a little differently. Allow yourself enough time to fully awaken before leaping out of bed. If it means setting the alarm clock a bit earlier, then do it. Before you set one foot out of bed, set the pace for your day by thanking whatever power you believe in for another sunrise, and another opportunity to truly live. Consciously take your time. Try not to think about being late. Think instead about the great things you'll accomplish today when you get to work. It doesn't matter if the only important thing you have to do that day is getting the paperwork cleared off of your desk. Think of the good things. Expect them. After all, the phone could ring with a new client on the other end of the line or an offer of a much better job.

Now, for those of you who are automobile commuters, comes the hard part. Even when you're stuck in traffic, even when people are cutting you off, even when your air conditioner decides to stop working, keep your cool. This culture we live in is one of hurry, hurry, hurry—and intense anxiety when we can't get our duties accomplished in the shortest possible time. Our freeways are maxed out, our public transit isn't sufficient, and we're practically a walking bleeding ulcer by the time we get to work.

We get to work and the deadlines loom. We have errands to run on the way home from work, the washer broke last night, and the dog needs to get to the vet. Before we know it we're in a sweat of anxiety, and we just don't know how to release it. We're worried about the rest of the day and we've only just begun living it.

The only way to get past this frenzy of stress is to take it one step at a time.

> *Me: "WHEN, Mom-Mom!!!"*
> *Edna: "When it's ready and not before."*

There truly is a time for every purpose under heaven. When you adjust that script in your mind, and begin accepting that there's a time, place, and reason for it all, you become relaxed. Why are you caught in a traffic jam? You may never know, but when you accept it, the adrenaline stops flowing and you become calm. Why are all your appliances breaking down at the same time? I don't know, but getting crazed over it will not help.

I've had more than a few people look at me and tell me I'm being too simplistic, that stress is just a part of modern life. I say, it doesn't have to be.

> *Edna said, "You've got to choose your battles, so choose the ones you can win. The only control I really have is over myself—not only my behavior but my reactions to*

others. If I react in an unpleasant way, I put another link in a chain of negative behavior that could stretch to the moon. Besides, it's more fun to kill people with kindness!"

Choose right this minute *not* to react. You don't have to jump for joy when the car needs new brakes and you don't have time to get it to the repair guy—but you do have to respond to the news without the adrenaline. You'll make better decisions. Your blood pressure will go down. You'll be a much happier and calmer person, too.

Think about what's important, and concentrate on that. Affirm that you'll have time to do all that needs to be done. Thinking about not having enough time or energy or money makes you crazy. Accept what the day brings. Affirm in your heart that you will accomplish all that needs to be done. Bless the day. Release it. You'll find a much happier you at the end of a busy day.

Put on thy strength

THE BOOK OF ISAIAH

5

Talk Is Not Cheap

*W*hen I was little, Edna told me "You know the
'Abracadabra' word in fairy tales? It's magic because it's an angel word, and it reminds you to always say
good things about others. The more good things you say,
the stronger your magic is."

Language is a gift. We convey so much with it. We speak
tender words of love to our families, we shout for someone to get
out of harm's way, and we have gentle, friendly conversation
over dinner with friends. Conversely, lack of language can convey fear or anger.

I have had the good fortune to read some wonderful New
Thought texts from the nineteenth century. One theme that
flows through them is the idea of the spoken word being a form
of magic. What we say influences our attitude and thoughts.

The words we say are so full of meaning, yet we tend to pay very
little attention to what's actually being uttered. How many words
do we say in a day? What is it that we are communicating to the
world? Many of us spend time accentuating the negative. It's hard
not to sometimes, but more often we don't even realize what we're
doing. Learning to take care in what we say is Step Three.

Talk Is Not Cheap

Look at our sometimes difficult world. Our lives go through cycles that appear to be out of control. Family and work grab the lion's share of our time, so much so that we have precious little time for ourselves. We're expected to be superpeople, and there aren't too many folks out there telling us how great we are. Sad, but true. Stress becomes a pattern.

What is stress? It's fear in a disguise. What do we do when we're fearful? We seek to protect ourselves, and sometimes that protection comes from complaining and fussing. Now, verbalizing our frustration is a good thing, as long as we are opening ourselves up, airing out the dirty laundry, learning from our difficulties, and then coming back to see things in a positive light. Fussing for the sake of fussing will do nothing but perpetuate your dissatisfaction.

> One day I was just generally out of sorts and cranky. Edna made me go outdoors and "look for delight." When she was feeling low she would go outside and find her pleasure in nature. She asked me to do the same, and then tell her what I saw. As soon as I started seeing beautiful things like the lilies of the valley that grew by her back door, and verbalized the feelings, my mood improved.
>
> "Speak beauty and you become it" is a phrase I found later in her letters.

Are you speaking beauty? Begin now to pay attention to your words. You might be a little surprised at what you hear. One of the biggest difficulties is to stop saying bad things about yourself. It may require some new training. As of right now, you must banish all the "I'm fat," I'm dumb," "I'm too old," and other self-defeating remarks from your vocabulary. This goes back to Step One. We can't clear out all that old negative stuff from our lives if we continue to verbalize it. Even something as seemingly innocuous as "God, I'm such a jerk" has the potential to be a land mine. Watch your words at all times. At first you'll be amazed at the things you say about yourself—and others! Once you become aware, you have the ability to remake your way of thinking and speaking.

You are your first project. All the abundance and peace of mind that is yours by birthright cannot begin to manifest until you love yourself. Loving yourself means not beating yourself up. We may have some deep emotional wounds to heal and the way to begin that healing is to state, quite clearly and out loud, that we love ourselves. Then we must prove it be refraining from words that will take us down.

> *"You can't get a turkey dinner out of a hamburger."*
> *(an Edna saying that was related later by Dad)*

You can't get turkey out of a hamburger, and you can't get a calm mind when stress and fear take over your language.

Be calm and loving with yourself, and then be that way with others. It's always possible to practice non-reaction. Non-reaction is letting unpleasantness wash over you like a wave, and then, like the wave, letting it retreat. When you have a choice between the nice thing to say and the unpleasant thing to say, choose the former. Gossip can be deadly. Do your best not to be a part of it.

Your workplace may be the area of your life that vexes you the most. Perhaps you're not crazy about everyone you work with, but you must be with them and be pleasant for at least 40 hours a week. When you're about to blow your stack, think of them as just being God's creatures doing their best. Practice non-reaction. You don't have to be a hypocrite, just don't react. You'll be pleasantly surprised to find that after a time, you'll not be as bothered by them as you were before. Even difficult supervisors respond to this treatment.

> *I was completely distressed one afternoon because a girl in my first-grade class decided that she "hated" me. I was lamenting to Edna, and she told me that most difficulties are "mind-tigers." I was puzzled, and so she had me draw a tiger on a sheet of paper. When I was done, she crumpled it up. "See? That tiger is made of paper, and I just crunched him up. Most problems are just like him. Don't worry, this will pass. Just don't be frightened."*
>
> *She was right.*

Life is full of paper mind-tigers. They can't bite you. You get to crunch them up by not feeding them with negative words.

In the rest of your world, try being more and more conscientious about the small niceties that make living more pleasant. Say "good morning" to those you see on the street. Compliment friends and co-workers when you sincerely admire something they've said or done. What comes around goes around, so you'll find yourself on the receiving end of more of this behavior, too. This will do wonders for your self-esteem, so you'll be much happier, and so on and so on in a delightful circle that just keeps increasing.

Does it seem too simple, the idea that words alone can begin to make a big impact on your life? We live in a complex world, and because of that we are trained to think that complex answers are needed to solve the riddles of life. It's a fib.

The path to understanding and enlightenment is lit by the simplest of lights. When this path begins to become illuminated, we cast light on our sorrows and difficulties as well. The attention brings them out of the gloom and into the open where they can be dealt with, and you can be free.

Thou hast enlarged my steps under me

THE BOOK OF II SAMUEL

6

Blessed Release

*W*hen I was six years old I made my stage debut, *such as it was, at Vacation Bible School. I sang "Jesus Loves Me" and "If You're Happy and You Know It." Edna was in the audience. When I got down from the performance platform she beamed at me and said "If you're happy and you know it the world is yours."*

Are you happy? Do your days contain more light than darkness? Have you learned and do you practice the gentle arts of compassion, humor, and forgiveness? If not, it's time to learn Catalyst Step number four. It's not as hard as you might think.

Blaming ourselves and others is the quickest way to the illusion of hell right here on earth. We tend to place blame when things don't go the way we've planned. This fault finding can manifest in one of two ways.

First, we can cast responsibility for our ills and unhappiness on those around us, fussing and raging and wasting precious energy. Think about what happens when you're angry with someone, blaming him or her for a situation that's not going well. You become preoccupied with thoughts of revenge and retribution. You become agitated. Tension can tie your body in knots, your stomach will become upset, your head might hurt.

All these symptoms from thoughts alone! We become so wrapped up in figuring out how to get even that we completely lose sight of contributions we could have made to the difficulty.

Alternatively, we can take the blame for everything that surrounds us, enveloping ourselves in quicksands of guilt. Blaming yourself and feeling guilty produce the same physical by-products. If we had a quarter for every "If only…" we've uttered or thought to ourselves! These "if onlys" are thoroughly toxic and keep us from living in the present. Self-recrimination and guilt forever drag us back to the past and put up massive roadblocks to our good thoughts and good health. We feel guilt right down to our toes. Guilt makes us feel frightened and vulnerable. It makes us second-guess ourselves. If you feel guilty, you always feel like your present actions have to make up for some action in the past. Talk about a treadmill! Forgiving yourself is the first step on a long road to a satisfied life.

When we cast blame, what we're really doing is cheating ourselves of the peacefulness that is ours by right.

> *"Forgive and forget, or live to regret."*

Being at peace is what we all strive for, and for many it's elusive. Why? There's something called the "race thought" that's frequently referred to in early and mid-twentieth century texts on New Thought. It has nothing to do with race as we currently think of it. Rather, it refers to the race between human beings, this whole of civilization we've made for ourselves and the thoughts contained therein. Race thought says that there is only a limited amount of success on this earth. It says that there is good and bad, and that all unpleasant things happen due to someone's error or laxity.

If we don't get what we're entitled to, maybe it's our boss or our mother's fault. Then again, maybe it's our fault. We can't provide all the things our family desires so we must either blame someone else or beat ourselves up over it.

This race thought also tells us in subtle and not so subtle ways that success is acquired through money, cars, houses, fancy toys, and all the outward trappings. Blame is a natural by-product of this kind of thinking. If we feel like we must follow along and follow the leader then we must acquire what the leader has to stay in the game. That still, small voice inside us is telling us what our life path is all the while, but the velocity of race thought keeps those quiet murmurs away from our range of hearing. We are taught that our intuition—that still, small voice—is just silly. We ignore the murmurings and follow along, because the promise is that as we live our lives, these things we acquire will make us happy and content.

What happens if the contentment doesn't come? You can make a decision to follow your happiness. What happens if guilt and blame are shed and the conscious mind makes a firm decision to follow the heart for pleasure and fulfillment? The life you were born to live is waiting for you to acknowledge it. Stories of dramatic mid-life career and life changes abound. Just from my own personal experience, I offer the following:

The lawyer who chucked his job to satisfy his desire to work with his hands. Carpentry and woodworking had been his life-long hobby, he was good at it, and within two years he had a thriving business.

The mid-level executive who felt empty and used up at the end of the workday. Her dream had been to own a restaurant. She went to culinary school, got a job as a chef, and within seven years of quitting her non-fulfilling job she opened the doors of her very own restaurant.

The young man who quit his father's very successful carpet business and went out to fulfill a dream of making music. He's not a star, but he's making quite a nice living, and he's fulfilling all of his creative urges.

Sometimes the way to contentment involves the biggest display of courage and faith you can muster. There's an alchemy that results when those two traits are combined, and the result is bravery. Courage will enable you to do those things that you may be fearful of, but bravery allows you to face those same daunting tasks with the full power of spirit behind and within you.

Have you heard of the power of "isness"? Isness says that all is well with the world, and that if we have a setback, we must have a lesson to learn from it somehow. Imagine how much insight you would acquire if mistakes and difficulties were looked at as windows of opportunity rather than situations full of blame. Living life in this fashion makes stress levels plummet and smiles abound. Taking responsibility builds character and tolerance.

*"God bless 'em, because I sure can't right now," Edna
would say on occasion when something unpleasant or un-
expected would happen. The frustration would never
last, though. She'd look at me and say, "Abracadabra.
God and I will both bless them."*

What about the times when someone truly hurts you on
purpose? It does happen, after all. Abracadabra. Know that
you have the means to break the negative chain. Take the high
road. Don't be a wimp, tell the person you've been hurt, but
walk away with no thought of revenge and then *let it go*. You'll
amaze those around you. You'll feel much better, and you'll win
in the end. Your heart—and most likely your body—will be
lighter.

Blame and guilt are blinders that keep us from seeing our
way through this world. Forgiveness is your goal, your path
through the race thought and on to a vision of a shining future.
Knowing what's true for you in this lifetime is the way to contentment. Kierkegaard said, "Life is lived forward but understood backward." For those who live their lives with blinders
on, that statement is true. By freeing ourselves from the karmic
nightmare of blame and guilt, however, we give ourselves the
means to understand and savor each step of our lives. We begin
to see not only with our eyes, but with our souls.

*Edna and I would walk around her property all the
time, just looking at flowers, trees, and wildlife. She*

would always ask me what I saw. One day, exasperated as only a child can be, I said, "Why do you keep asking me the same question?" Edna looked at me and said "New eyes see much more clearly, my dear. Perhaps I can see through you something that I've missed."

Awake up, my glory

THE BOOK OF PSALMS

7

Love-a-Dub-Dub

In the 50s, one of Edna's friends was getting ready to divorce her husband. It was known that Anna* wanted to marry someone else. At that time, in a small town, those things were pretty outrageous. When most other people in town turned their backs on Anna, Edna did not. She made it a point to invite both her and her new husband to dinner frequently. Why? "Anna had the guts to walk out the door of misery into a life of love and contentment. Bully for her. She's a hero as far as I'm concerned."

Anna and her new husband lived happily ever after, by the way.

The Beatles say that all we need is love. That's not exactly true. We need love, faith, and guts to see all the joy that is meant for us in this life.

Getting to love is the last of the Catalyst Steps. It means getting out of fear and hate. When you boil it down, hate is really just fear all dolled up in a different outfit. If we hate someone or something, it always has a basis in fear. When we

---
* *a pseudonym*

48

hate a person, we're afraid that they'll hurt us, take our job away, or take something that is ours. If they're a different race or religion, we may be afraid because we don't understand their culture. It's a peculiar fact of this world we live in that most people find it easier to avoid and condemn something they don't understand rather than try to learn more and accept.

Do you recognize those moments in your life when everything seems possible? You know what I'm talking about. Those days when the sky seems bluer, people you meet on the street are friendlier, you feel like a million bucks and you feel like you could conquer the world? Think back to the last time that happened to you. What you felt was a heart expansion. Joy and love for every single thing filled your mind. Any room for fear and hate in there? I don't think so!

Love and hate are two emotions that will cancel each other out. The choice is up to you. By basing our daily lives on hate and fear, we draw the storm clouds that sap our zest for life. How do you feel when fear is present? Like there's a vacuum cleaner pressed up to your guts sucking all the life force out of you. Scared and nervous, that's what we not only become, but also what we project to the world. Love and acceptance are the furthest things from our minds. Have you noticed that whenever you feel fearful, the good things in life don't seem to happen to you? At those times we've pushed the positive so far away from us that all we have left to experience is difficulty. When you are in a fear state, all instincts are for self-protection. We become very thin-skinned and defensive. Looking for the negative becomes the norm, along with suspicion and cynicism. The optimum goal is a life that is joyous—when we become frightened we start existing rather than truly living, and we begin attracting all the wrong stuff.

Let's talk about hate and fear. Rather, let's talk about getting rid of them. Make a decision—right this minute—to let go of them completely. Hate poisons the body. If you hate someone, what happens when you think of or see them? You feel your blood pressure go up, you get anxious, you feel tempted to say unpleasant things. In other words, your body clutches and falls into "fight mode." You may not actually have a verbal or physical fight, but your body reacts in much the same way. So...who loses? You. You don't have to be buddies with everyone you meet, but you <u>do</u> have to have at least a neutral attitude. Hatred and fear eat at the emotional, spiritual, and physical parts of ourselves. It's too much of a price to pay.

You always have a choice. Do you realize this? Right now, you can choose to look at the world with a peaceful eye. As human beings, we are deciders. We decide how we're going to feel about a given situation. Absolutely any event in your life can be looked at in a myriad of ways. If you choose to view difficulties as opportunities to learn rather than catastrophes, you begin to win this game called Life. Others may look at you as if you've gone off the deep end— after all, crying and wailing are expected! Moving out of fear-based decision making is your goal. When you do this, everyday living becomes easier and easier. This is not a platitude—it's the truth. When you give up an attachment to poisonous thoughts, life becomes a joy.

Since hate and fear go hand in hand, what is the companion to love? In a word, peace. With a life based on love and peacefulness, there's a sense of pleasure in the day, even if it's filled with duties like running to the supermarket and the dry cleaners. There is a sense of wonderful positive expectation, like absolutely anything terrific could happen at any time. Best of all, many times it does. Positive expectation creates an atmosphere of happiness and magic. When you are in a peaceful state, this becomes a natural mindset. You feel great, you look great, and you can't help but smile. Pour your love out to the world, and it comes back to you tenfold!

> *Flowers and bees*
> *And puppies and trees*
> *Make me just one thing*
> *That's happy!*

> *(Edna's Happy Song, which as a child I sang repeatedly at the top of my lungs whenever possible.)*

"Love everyone?" you say. "How can I love someone if I don't really know them, or if they've been cruel to me?"

The emotion of love is strong, rich, and deeply varied. It can be the love of a wife for her husband or of a mother for her child. There's a much larger piece of the puzzle, however. Think of the love that Jesus and Gandhi had for their fellow man. We know of the peacefulness of their lives. What a wonderful model!

Love others as a part of this great big human race, as another person doing his or her very best, just like you. When you do that, you automatically become more empathetic and understanding. We're all here, at various stages of enlightenment, learning and doing all we can.

Opening your mind to possibilities is the avenue out of the world of stinky thoughts. Just as difficult states of mind seem to expand and multiply, so do positive states of mind. We just don't notice it as much. Edna said that it's easier to create drama with bad news, so that's why people dwell on it so much. She also said she had "quite enough drama in her life as it was, thank you," and that she'd "stick with the good stuff."

"Good stuff" means loving the world. It does not, however, mean that you're supposed to let people walk all over you, take advantage of you, and treat you poorly. It is having the courage of your convictions. You don't ever have to be hateful or unpleasant. Take the high road. Extricate yourself from an unpleasant circumstance or relationship, wish the other person love, and simply go on your way.

At some point in history, someone decided that life was supposed to be difficult and full of trouble. This person must have had a very good press agent because before long, the world became convinced of this. This false truth has been around for too long, and now it's time to smash it. Life is supposed to be good. It's not supposed to be full of difficulty. Release blame and fear. Take responsibility. Look at the world with love in your eyes. Look at *yourself* with that same love. Prove the naysayers wrong.

Grab this life and live it, as Edna did.

Just be yourself, no matter what those around you say. Use your love with boldness and wisdom, and no power will take advantage of you.

> *One of Edna's philosophies: "Life is meant to be fun. If you don't have any fun you're missing the point."*

I wholeheartedly agree.

Let not your heart be troubled

THE BOOK OF JOHN

8

What Will People Think? (who cares?)

My grandmother's family came to America in the eighteenth century. The Larsons, my grandfather's family, were a much more recent arrival from Sweden, and the cultural differences between the two families were vast. I asked Edna one day how she came to marry my grandad, Ivar. She told me that she fell in love immediately and they had eloped. Being a kid, I said, "Oooh, was your Mom mad?" Edna looked me squarely in the eye and said, "Baby, I never cared. And no one has had a better life than me. Trust your heart and you'll always win. The whole purpose of life is to live it, love it, and take a happy smile to God when you're done. I never gave a hoot about what anyone thought."

And do you know what? Every member of my family, both Larsons and Tilghmans, adored her.

Isn't it true that we spend a lot of time wondering what others think of us?

One of my teachers said the most marvelous thing to me years ago—"What you think of me is none of my business." I chuckled at the time, and he very seriously told me that his life was lived according to that principle. I'll never forget that phrase, mostly because it reminded me so much of Edna.

Edna somehow knew as a young girl that this life was meant to be seized and lived to the fullest. Apparently she did not have to go through the "what will people think?" phase. From all accounts she was calm the anchor for many in our family, and was never swayed by outward appearances.

My grandmother was a true and steadfast believer in Spirit. She had been introduced to affirmative prayer by a friend. She credited this "very pleasant habit" with her ability to be steadfast, kind, and resistant to the negativity of others. She also just happened to be akin to the Rock of Gibraltar, and everyone who knew her was aware of the affirmations that made her this way. If you're not acquainted with this idea and way of living, I'll give you an introduction.

Affirmative prayer is about rejoicing and thanksgiving. It's recognizing all the wonder, joy, and abundance in your life and being thankful from the bottom of your heart. This way of life does not involve beseeching prayer—it's more like a meditation, a communion with Spirit. This kind of prayer affirms perfection in our lives as we are thankful for having received all that we need, even if it hasn't shown up quite yet.

It's about faith.

Faith can be hard to come by, and when we march to a different drummer, our spirit can be taxed and sometimes on the edge of despair. This is when following your own tune and not worrying about what others think can be the most difficult.

Edna taught me about faith and resistance to others' negative views by telling me about what I earlier referred to as the race thought—the thought pattern that underlies much of human behavior in a not-so-positive way—though she did not describe it as such. She said that many people live with the illusion that life happens from the outside in. This way of looking at the world results in a life that is lived on the surface, rather than from the inside.

> *"If you're on the inside looking out, you get to see everything!" Edna said. "Trying to check things out from the outside is much more difficult—the windows tend to be mirrored and they distort any images we might see."*

When you want something, what do you do? You move in a forward motion. How many times have good things appeared to you that seem to be just on the other side of a big glass door? You can see it, you can smell it, you can even hear it, but it's just out of reach. Most people push against the door with all their might. They push harder and harder, and that door just stays shut. The more they push, the less that door is going to budge. They are pushing from the outside, trying to get to all their good.

What if I told you that the door to living successfully opens inward? And that your good is waiting for you to simply allow the door to open on its own?

Most folks react with a sharp intake of breath when I tell them that. We're taught to be aggressive, to always move forward and never take a step back. Allow? We don't allow, we pursue! We're told to model ourselves after the successful members of our society. We do what's currently accepted as fashionable and acceptable. Being stressed and constantly on the go takes up all of our time. We're taught in our society that we have to do certain things to fit in. We face tremendous pressure to conform, to keep up with the Joneses.

(As my father would say: "Who are these Jones people? Are they really that happy? And are you sure you want to be like them?")

We don't have to keep up with anyone. Life is about being thankful for what you have and what you're about to receive. It's about keeping the negative comments from others away from your heart. It's about listening to that still, small voice within us. It's about living a happy life. A happy life contains abundance from many sources, and your path to abundance may be a lot different than another's. Celebrate the differences. Achieve balance.

Balance. How do you get it? Balance is achieved by right thinking. Right thinking is achieved by following your own internal compass. Impressions and opinions come from everywhere—parents, friends, the guy down the street. Frustration and imbalance often come when we try to reconcile our wants and needs with the wants of others, those who "have our best interests at heart." Our loved ones have good intentions, but no one can know the right path for you but you. Balance comes when you love yourself enough to put your own needs first. Loving yourself has nothing to do with narcissism. It's a deep feeling of self-respect. With that self-respect comes the ability to forge your own path with joy.

When we hold others' opinions in high esteem, we have a constant battle of emotions. The "shoulds" and "wants" are at war. We alternate between periods of satisfaction and self-doubt. Some of us can be immobilized, and spend years stuck on hold, trying to reconcile our deep knowing with the expectations of those around us. By commanding self-respect and by giving respect to others, we neutralize those mood swings that threaten to overwhelm us.

There's an old expression—"one's ship comes in over a calm sea." Your life path and attendant abundance will materialize when your internal sea is calm and centered. Nothing can land safely if your emotions are crashing about like storm waves on the rocks. What does a ship do in a storm? It stays away from shore, as the unpredictable waves can send it crashing into the cliffs. Think of your abundance as that ship. All that is yours by right and divinity is waiting, just offshore, for the emotions to balance. When the storms pass, all will become clear.

Do you have balance in your life? Edna was the most balanced woman I've ever known, and she took the time to live every moment as it came. She would weigh the opinion of others, but toss it out if it ran contrary to what her heart was telling her. She was so completely at ease with herself that everyone she came in contact with felt at ease as well. She said it was because she followed the Golden Rule every day of her life.

The Golden Rule—treat others as you wish to be treated. It was the reason she suffered very few slings and arrows. Even if others disagreed with her, she was never cruel or unpleasant to them. She let them have their opinion and went on her merry way. It didn't matter what others thought, only that she be treated with respect. By showing everyone around her that same respect, even if they disagreed with her, she commanded that respect in return. Edna mastered the art of living by treating others as she wished to be treated herself.

We don't all have to be the same. Balance comes when we cut ourselves loose from that idea. Every single one of us was born to do something special on this earth, something no one else can do in exactly the same way. To go within, to find this source, is our highest ideal. Allow the door to your good to open...inward. Remain aware that we are all on the same path, which is the path to finding ourselves. If we can be kind to each other on the way, we'll all arrive much sooner, and with fewer bruises! By allowing others to be themselves, we can expect the same in return, and we won't obsess over the opinions of others. This attitude of calm will illuminate your soul, bringing on the peace and light of a balanced life.

Edna said that human beauty can be seen by the light of the soul, not the light of the sun. Even in darkness, someone who is filled with that light is instantly recognizable.

"Treat everyone, no matter who it is, the way you wish to be treated, and your life will be made of gold."

According to your faith be it unto you

THE BOOK OF MATTHEW

9

Turning Mud into Chocolate

Edna always made me feel strong and smart. When I was really little I used to make the usual mudpies. She would ooh and ahh over them and put them in the freezer. She would say, "Now we can't open the freezer for a week, it has to set up. No peeking or it will be ruined."

The next week she'd have a chocolate cupcake on the very same plate waiting for us in the freezer. We'd go get it together, and eat it on the sunporch.

"How did you make this mud taste so good?" she would ask. "You must give me the recipe."

How do some people always manage to see the good in life? Who are those people who can make chocolate cupcakes out of mudpies? Why is it that some people can find healing easily and others can't?

These questions are huge, so complex and yet so simple. The answer is this: there's always a price to pay. You're saying "Aha! I knew there was a catch!" Well...not exactly. The price is easy to come by, but because of the way most of society is programmed, it can be quite a struggle to pay it.

Turning Mud into Chocolate

Here it is: you must be willing to give up negative and self-abusive thought forms and actions. Your goal is to improve your thinking, slowly but surely weeding out the old patterns and replacing them with new, positive, and loving attitudes. That means, simply, to get out of hate and fear, and into love and peaceful co-existence.

It sounds wonderful and easy, but in the beginning it can be an uphill battle. The reason has nothing to do with you as a person—it's the way we were raised and the world we live in today.

As an experiment, do this. Next time you have lunch with a group of friends and co-workers, listen to the conversation like a researcher. Note the negatives that are discussed as well as the positives. Pay close attention. The negatives usually win. Negatives are anything that puts anyone or anything down. Even something as seemingly innocuous as "I hate my hair" or "she's driving me crazy" is fuel for the negativity game.

Getting into positive mode from a negative one is the basis of a joyful life. It takes mindfulness. It takes awareness. It takes commitment.

How to get started? You're possibly thinking that all you have to do is recite affirmations, meditate, and be kind to everyone you meet. This is where a lot of self-help books and tapes miss the mark. Affirmations, meditations, and kindness are all extremely important, but they can't get you where you want to go without two very important ingredients: belief in yourself and balance.

Belief in the power to create the life you want is the engine that fires everything you do in life, including all the wonderful things that you do for yourself. Sincere belief is, quite simply, magic.

The truth is that it's the most important—and probably most difficult—challenge of your life. Changing deep-seated patterns and images requires strength, faith, patience, and, most importantly, self-love. Self-love does not mean narcissism. It means having a deep abiding respect for yourself, for this unique creature that was born to do something on this Earth that no one else can do. It means overcoming the hurtful stabs of nastiness and unwarranted criticism that come from others. It means listening to your own inner guides, safe and secure in the knowledge that you can create your own reality.

Balance comes from an appropriate amount of work, play and meditation. Working all the time makes us crazy, tired and spiritually depleted. Our culture has become one of workaholics—we're expected to work superhuman hours, and then manage to wedge a family, friends and some leisure time into the precious few hours that are left. We need to find the time to do something fun *without* feeling guilty. We can't change our frenzied work lives overnight, but we can change our way of thinking. We can take the time to do something nice for ourselves, even if it's just thirty minutes in a café savoring a cup of tea and a croissant and, above all, relaxing. Your good can't flow in over all the static of tension.

Those who have learned how to make the most of their lives

also have the power of meditation at their disposal. You don't have to have incense and candles and tons of time. All you need is ten completely uninterrupted minutes in the morning and at night. Lock yourself in the bathroom if you have to. Take—*insist*—on this time. Relaxation and meditation make ways for the scales of life to balance again. Doing a bit of both of them every day will take the rough edges away, allowing you to see some of the hidden capabilities lurking inside you. Constant work creates constant static, a feeling of dashing about in this life without really living. Balance can be achieved by introducing moments, and then minutes, of calm into your day.

Open yourself up to the flow of creativity and healing, both conventional and alternative. This action begins to open up the Godlike portions of yourself that may be hidden away. Oneness is the source of health, and to me oneness means keeping body, mind, and spirit together.

The bottom line is this—love is *it*. I'm not being simplistic. As you learn the Catalyst Steps, you'll see the effects of love and hate on your life as you now live it. Your eyes will be opened, and the opportunity for change and healing will be there for you to take advantage of at any time. Love. Edna had a lot to say on the subject.

> *Edna on self-love.* "We're taught to love our neighbor as ourselves. Then many of us are taught that we're a bunch of lousy sinners, dependent only on mercy for a shot at an afterlife devoid of fire and brimstone. Well, well. This is only my opinion, mind you, but that is the

biggest bunch of hooey I ever heard. How can I love myself if I'm taught continually that I'm no good and someone has to save me?"

Before we can love anyone or anything, we have to learn to love ourselves. I know that for many of us, this journey is a long and arduous one. We've had too many people telling us for far too long just how fat, dumb, clumsy, weak, etc., we are. Human beings are very suggestible. When we hear these things over and over again, we start to believe them. We are what we believe. After a time, we actually do start to exhibit clumsiness, or put on too many pounds. It's because we begin to believe these things that people say to us. It's not true. We just hear it so much we begin to assume it is.

When we add overwork to the mixture, life gives the appearance of being out of control. The truth is that you can begin to regain control at any time. Decide to claim your life, this fabulous opportunity to be the best you can be.

Turn your belief into belief in yourself, not belief in your inability to measure up. Put aside the comments of others and find your center, that place of complete balance. Ignite that knowledge that you can do what you want and be who you want to be. Remember what it was like when you were a child, and every possibility was open to you? Go to that place again. Feel that freedom.

It's from that place of power that you can turn any old mudpies in your world into the finest chocolate.

Sow abundantly and ye shall reap abundantly

THE BOOK OF II CORINTHIANS

10

Making the Most of It All

I used to complain, as all kids do, that it seemed I would never grow up. On my ninth birthday, just before Edna died, I got this note from her in my birthday card:

"...*You'll be grown up in about a minute, and I want to give you my recipe for success in life. Success is making yourself happy, which will in turn open the path to making others happy. Love yourself, and remember that time passes much too quickly. Don't waste a moment. Take what you've learned from me and from others and be a grand girl! PS Save me some cake.*"

As a nine year old, I completely blew this off and went for the present, of course. Those words that she wrote me that day started to make sense only when I became an adult, and realized life in "grown-up time." In "kid time," it seems to take twenty years to get from one birthday to another. Grown-up time means the process reverses itself, and twenty years pass by in the blink of an eye.

It seems that as a society we've forgotten how to make ourselves happy. Madison Avenue would have us believe that joy comes from acquisition, from constantly buying the newest and latest. What have we learned in the hundred years of modern advertising—that things go better with a certain soft drink? Is it really true that using a particular antiperspirant will encourage a marriage proposal? And, hey—is it true that those who have hair of a golden hue have more fun? You may be thinking, "Silly old advertising jingles, that's all they are." True, but some of those silly old jingles have been in my head for at least *three decades*. That's the kind of effect advertising can have. Constant repetition creates tape loops that are mighty hard to get away from.

What are the tape loops in your mind right now? I don't mean commercials, I mean the negative things we say to ourselves that undermine the success and joy that are ours by birthright. Don't forget these unpleasant things that others have said about us that we have taken to heart. Are these still playing in the undercurrent of your consciousness, subtly affecting the choices and decisions you make?

The advertising analogy is a good one, because it shows how deeply a phrase or belief can become ingrained in your mind. It may not always be at the top of your consciousness, but it's there, lurking about, waiting for the correct prompt to bring it to the surface.

It is human nature to hang onto things, file them away for future reference. We can't help but be information gatherers—it's part of the way we live. In the twentieth century, this gathering has gotten completely out of control. Why? We live in the information age. We are exposed to more information in one day than Edna was exposed to in a year. We feel like we have to stay on top of everything, and never let anything get away. Storage and maintenance of this information becomes a full time job. We don't have time for friends and relaxation— Gotta run! Gotta go!

When we take the time to breathe, we see the hollow world we've created for ourselves. Where are our friends? Real friends, the ones who will be there for us no matter what? Do we have any? If not, where did they go? Friendship requires information gathering of the most basic kind, and that's simply gathering information about another person's likes and dislikes, desires and dreams. Friendship takes time. Knowing that I have someone like my childhood friend Chris, for example, makes the highs in my life much more glorious, and makes the lows much easier to take. Friendship is as essential to humanity as air, food and water. Without it, we feel alone and misunderstood. Contact with other human beings is the only way to guarantee even a modicum of happiness in this life.

"My mother always said that true love comes from the deepest place in your heart, but I think that's only halfway true. If we love from only the heart, we don't know how to handle the hurts when they come along. If we love from the spirit as well as the heart, we understand the grand plan, and know that the small hurts we endure are actually lessons we must learn. Hard lessons

sometimes, that's for sure, but learning them brings us closer to God. Contrary to what people may think, the heart never breaks. It becomes more pliant and more able to love with each lesson learned."

What is a spiritual crisis? It usually means that we feel separate from God, from that feeling of oneness with the Universe. We feel alone, sometimes helpless, and always misunderstood. How do we get to that point of crisis? We still have these negative tape loops lurking in our subconscious from ages ago. We can be doing quite well, happy in our lives and careers, and all of a sudden it feels like the bottom has just dropped out of our carefully built house of life. The bottom drops out because our hearts—and our spirits—are asking us to pay attention. Those tapes need to be erased. We can live an ordinary life in an ordinary way for just so long—then our true nature starts to call out to us. The call comes in unsettling ways for those who are not prepared. The call shakes us to our very bones, and the question is this: What is the meaning of life?

Everyone from philosophers and priests to bartenders and shopkeepers have been examining and arguing this question for centuries. Millions of pounds of paper have been committed to scholarly theses on the subject. We ponder and argue and search, and the answer is right smack inside of us, in our heart-space.

The meaning of life is this: It is Love.

Eeek! you say. That's too easy and it's silly besides. Take a peek backwards right now and look at the Catalyst Steps, and read again about love. Approach life with an attitude of love. When you do this, you will automatically be in a forgiving and accepting frame of mind. When you can move forward without the barriers of fear and suspicion, you are in a state of love, also known as a state of grace. A state of grace can instantly erase all of the old, unpleasant images you have of yourself and the false beliefs about your (lack of) ability. Remaining in a state of grace can prevent them from returning.

A state of grace can occur anytime, anywhere, and it happens in personal and business relationships. Let's face it, there are many situations that make us a little nuts by the injustice of it all. What happens when you look at the situation from a state of grace? You accept that it has happened, you calmly think about ways to fix or change it, and you go on your way. No fussing or raging is necessary. Your intuition is your personal guidebook, and it can be accessed easily when you remain centered. Using your intuition allows you to make the most of any situation in which you find yourself.

A state of grace (or love) is what we're all searching for. Mid-life is the time when a lot of this searching comes to the forefront. "Mid-life crisis" it's called, but it doesn't have to be a crisis. All the hopes and dreams you've been carrying for years come to the fore at this time of life. You may have achieved many great things, made tons of money, and have a beautiful home, but have you followed the spiritual side of your nature? I'm not just talking about your personal life here—how about your business life? No matter how successful you are, if you're not doing things that you're passionate about, it doesn't mean much. We tell ourselves that it's OK as long as we make enough money and give a few bucks away here and there. "Grow up!" you say to yourself. "Not everyone is lucky enough to get to do what he wants with his life, so I'll just shut up, do my job, and make the mortgage."

I will tell you right now that this is a guaranteed way to deaden your emotions, and it puts you on a collision course with despair. Of course we can't just quit our jobs and become instant golf pros, but we can take steps to do the things we want to do. It is NEVER too late.

Spiritual crises come when we have given up our dreams. Whatever those dreams may be, pursue them any way you can. Be creative, and be fearless. Look at the big picture of your life.

Here's an exercise for you. Find a comfortable chair, turn off the phone, close your eyes, and daydream about your life. Assume that you have enough money to do what you wish to do, so none of your daydreams will be about survival or making money. Everything you do, you do for love. What would your day be like? What would a typical week be like? Think about this in depth, and carry your life daydream right up to very old age. See yourself doing all the things you want to do. Don't be afraid to include time for relaxation as well. Our culture is trained to work like dogs, and frankly, that's not the way to good health of body, mind, and spirit. In this daydream, you can sit on the beach for two hours just staring at the water if you want to.

After you've spent some time at this exercise, begin writing things down. The high spots. The things that gave you goosebumps when you thought of them. Look at that piece of paper and realize that those activities will bring you closer to the state of grace we all crave. These are the activities our hearts encourage us to pursue, and the solution is to just...begin.

We are our own worst enemies and critics. Humans tend to crave security, and radical change can be threatening. We also have a tendency to project and not take things one day at a time. We get so frightened of potential catastrophes that we go rushing back to our shells and close them up tight. If we think of taking pottery lessons, for instance, we start thinking about the drive, and what if we're late, and what if it snows, and what if the instructor doesn't like us, and what if we're not as good as the others in the class and on and on and on. Before we know it, in our minds we've failed so we figure we should just forget about it.

Take life one day at a time. We hear this phrase repeatedly, but do we apply it? So many good things happen to us and we don't even take the time to notice them. Check out that gorgeous blue sky. Feel the texture of the lovely sweater you have on today that makes you feel so beautiful when you wear it. Say hello to that dear doorman who greets you by name every morning. Appreciate the kiss your husband and kids give you in the morning before they're off to whatever their day has in store for them. Alternatively, if you're having a difficult day, don't rage at the world. Look at the difficulties with a clear eye. Did you contribute to the problem? If so, take responsibility and tell yourself to change your approach in the future. If you didn't contribute to the problem, think of ways to avoid conflict in the future. Either way, look on the experience as a *lesson*.

> *"There is something that is being awakened in the souls of all of us. I won't live long enough to see it, but you will. Use your light to help others find the way."*

Unpleasant things do not happen to us because we're bad people. They just plain happen. Every obstacle, challenge, or problem is simply a small setback on this road of life. Life is series of lessons. Learn the lesson, and get promoted. Don't learn the lesson and, guess what? You're doomed to repeat it. Open your mind, open your eyes, and let spirit shine through all you do.

Learn, grow, and make the most of this gift of life. We are all divine beings—we just haven't learned how to pierce the veil of illusion, the veil that has us all thinking that we have no control over our lives. We do. Use your power to create the world that you want. You have the ability. Find your courage, use good judgement, and achieve a state of grace. By doing that, you will truly be making the most of this fabulous experience called life.

Whatsoever you desire, believe that you have received, and you shall have it

THE BOOK OF MARK

11

Have I Got an Adventure for You...

Edna stopped going to church when she got married and no longer had to obey her father's rules. "My church is outside my backdoor," she would say. "My heaven is in my heart. I know most people don't understand me, but I have a deep sense of knowing my place in this world. The power of earth and spirit is deeply divine."

There's an old saying that life is a gift to be opened and enjoyed every single day—that's why they call it the present.

There is purpose and order to this world. It's time to open our eyes and see living for what it really is—an opportunity to grow, learn, and most of all, revel in this gift of life. When life is seen as the powerful learning experience it is meant to be, suddenly everything will change. Your outlook on life will expand to a range you never thought possible. The peace in your heart will be reflected in your life. You'll be healthier, look better, and feel years younger. Why? Because the false idea that life is a burden will have been lifted from your shoulders.

I'd love to know the exact time period in history when life ceased being a pleasure and became a chore. Too many people on this earth are living their lives under the erroneous impression that that's the way it's supposed to be. Somehow the message that life is a great and wonderful journey of learning got turned around, and millions of people live lives of dissatisfaction—sometimes downright misery—with the hope that the afterlife will bring them relief. The idea that toiling and suffering today will be exchanged for rewards in the next world made Edna crazy.

> *While my dad was not a natural healer, he certainly did respect his mother Edna used to tell him stories of the Depression, when everyone was suffering and praying for decent crops so the family could at least eat. Dad told me that Edna knew her family would survive and thrive, and that's exactly what happened. She said to him, "My family never faced poverty, because Mother believed in the goodness of life and of Heaven. She had firm faith that we would make it through with all we needed and then some And we did! I even got to finish college. Mother believed, and so did the rest of us."*

What is it that makes the difference in our lives? Why do some people demonstrate health and abundance and others are struggling from day to day? It comes down to freedom from fear and the belief that we truly can create our own destiny.

The prophet Solomon said "with all thy getting, get understanding." I take this to mean that the world must be understood on its own terms. Here's where the adventure begins! It's an adventure because all too often we must ride the waves of others' opinions and overcome the seeming reality that surrounds us. We can get all the material things in the world, but if we don't understand the meaning of it all, we can still be disillusioned and depressed. Do you have what you want in this life? Are you finding your road to health, prosperity, and happiness? If not, let's talk about why not.

First and foremost, nature operates in cycles. We see it very clearly in those areas of the world that have four distinct seasons. In Washington, DC, where I live, we have the advantage of seeing the cycle of life played out every single year. Spring brings new growth, with flowers happily pushing their way out of the ground and trees full of buds. Summer brings lush growth, blooming flowers, and plenty of sunshine. Fall comes, and the plants begin to pull their life force back towards the roots. Leaves fall from the trees, squirrels put away food for the winter, and the days begin to get shorter. Winter brings cold and seeming bleakness. Bare trees are far from lifeless, however. All the energy is stored in the roots, resting, waiting for the warmth of Spring to release it all over again. Even in more temperate climates we see the cycles of plant and animal life, just not quite so dramatically.

If nature has this cycle, and we as living beings are a part of nature, it only stands to reason that we have this same cycle. If a plant ceases to grow and change, it dies. The same thing happens to human beings, only it's our souls that seem to die.

We've been conditioned to be afraid of change. We must

constantly strive to learn, know, and be more than we have been previously. To do that is to stretch our spirit, and it puts us in contact with the divine that resides in all of us. The patterns we've made over the years can become as soothing as our favorite comforter. We snuggle up inside and keep the rest of the world at bay. We're cozy and warm, but if we stay curled up in that comforter we'll never experience new opportunities and growth.

What happens when the world you've built for yourself doesn't quite fit anymore? For many of us, fear keeps us from stepping outside of the boundaries we've erected. I've heard so many people say, "Well, better the devil I know than the devil I don't know." Such words bring on stagnation, because they signify a lack of willingness to grow, stretch and ultimately prosper. This fear of expanding our comfort zone can paralyze us and keep us from the ultimate expression of our life on earth.

When a plant has an opportunity to grow, it stretches toward the heavens to show off the new buds. Too many times we, as human beings, have the opportunity to grow, and we hide our heads. Imagine if nature did that. The world would be turned upside down.

The road away from your fear and into an expanded life is one of spiritual thinking. This way of thinking changes you from the inside out. It involves the combination of faith, courage and action.

Spiritual thinking means being in a state of expanded consciousness. What do I mean by that? Let Edna say it:

"If I expect miracles, I get them. By opening my mind to the endless possibilities of life, I guarantee that I will experience all the good that's mine by right. We do have a right to happiness, you know. I wish everyone would realize that."

The way out of your troubles begins with you. This book contains principles and suggestions for living a life that's more joyful and fulfilling. By reading this book, you start the wheels of progress turning. Once your mind is tuned into a new frequency, a world of possibilities awaits. The next step is action. Here's your challenge.

Take a step away from the seeming reality around you. You may have been telling yourself that you're too old to do something, perhaps going back to school or changing jobs. Turn your back on limiting words and begin thinking about what you would do if you could change your life. What school would you go to? What would you major in? What would your dream job be like? Where would you live?

Get a small notebook or journal and write down the answers to these questions. Be specific and do not, by any means, limit your thinking. There are no barriers—in this journal you can do and be whatever you wish. Be as precise as you can. Write about the job you want in detail. Describe not only the area in which you wish to live, but describe your house as well. Write about the yard, the rose bushes, the drapes, whatever you wish. You are beginning to create the world of your dreams, and there is no detail too small to be included.

Don't forget to write about how you are feeling in this new world you've created for yourself. See yourself as living your dream. Describe your contentment, excitement, or pleasure. If you have difficult relationships with anyone in your life, see and feel them as warm and positive. If your mate is driving you mad, visualize and describe a lovely day together, enjoying yourselves and being free of arguments and strife. A sense of delight and peace will be with you as you write all of these images down.

As you commit this new life to paper, I want you to become it. Think about what you are wearing, the tea you are drinking, whether you're sitting inside or on the porch. Feel the breeze in your hair, or the warmth of the fire in the fireplace. Live the experience as you write it down. Feel the emotions that are stirred as you write about and visualize the life you've always dreamed of.

Take your time, and be as complete as possible. Make sure you leave a few blank pages because as you read and re-read your description of a perfect life, you'll add to it. It never fails! No matter how complete we think our essay is, there's always another bit of happiness we can add at a later date.

The next part of the mission is to keep track of the ways in which you are bringing your perfect life about. Set goals – small ones to start. If you want to go back to school, start sending for catalogs. If you want to move, get in touch with the Chamber of Commerce in a few different cities and get information. Start shaping up that resume, if changing jobs is your desire. The thing to remember is that the door to your good opens inward. Make your plans, do what needs to be done, then step back and allow it to happen.

> *"Every day there are little miracles. Find them, see them. That way, you'll never be tempted to look back. If you keep going forward, you will ultimately get what you desire."*

Every single day is filled with potential. Edna told me to look for signs of Spring. She didn't mean the season, she meant Spring in my heart! The signs and symbols of the Spring season are subtle—the air smells different, you'll see a robin in the distance, or a crocus begins to shoot up out of the ground. The signs of your own Spring, the beginning of the rest of your new (and improved) life come in the very same way. Let's say you want to move to San Francisco. You'll find yourself noticing articles about that city, or photos of the Golden Gate Bridge. You may find that you stumble across a documentary about it on public television, or a new friend mentions that she'd gone there recently. These are all ways to tell that your message is being worked on by that greatest of powers—your very own. Put the thought out there, be strong and unwavering, and it will surely be drawn directly to your door.

Of course, we have free will. You may actually draw the opportunity right up to your nose, and then lack the guts to go through with it. Be specific in what you ask for, but plan to get it. Sometimes it comes quickly. Be prepared. Live in that state of positive expectation

As you experience the signs of Spring in your own life, you'll begin to understand the great truth, that life is here to be lived and enjoyed. We have the ability to create heaven on earth if we are brave. Being brave means to stand firm when others attempt to bring you down. Being aware of the world around you and finding miracles is a joy beyond compare, but there are those who may challenge you, and attempt to belittle or make fun of you.

Stand firm.

The knowledge and experience of happiness is open to all who have the courage to claim it. Be one of those people. Understand your capacity to heal your life. Your self-awareness will make others want to share in the light, even the ones who may have made fun of you!

Join me on this marvelous adventure, making our lives all that we desire. No one can give us our dreams, we have to give them to ourselves. Put away the strife and fear, and come into love and creation. Believe that you can. Edna would have been so pleased.

Ye are the light of the world

THE BOOK OF MATTHEW

12

Affirmations for Positive Fulfillment

"*If you don't speak your mind, how in the world will I know what it is that you want?*"

Life would have been so much easier for me if Edna had been around during my adolescent and young adult periods. As a child, she taught me to speak my mind. As I got older, I was taught to "keep my own counsel," as they say. I wished and prayed for things, but more often than not these prayers were not answered in the way that I wanted. I couldn't figure it out. Finally, I opened my mouth. I remembered what she had said:

> "*Wishing and hoping are fine if you want things to remain just wishes and hopes. To make them real, you've got to use your voice. It's the magic that a lot of people forget to use!*"

It's difficult for some of us to come up with prayers and affirmations. We know what we want, we just don't necessarily know what to say! Being prayerfully tongue-tied isn't such an awful thing—you just need a little push in the right direction. You'll get the hang of it, and then there's no stopping you, especially when you begin to see those prayers being answered.

I've written some of my favorite affirmations here for you to use, or to use as a guide to write your own. Use them frequently. Write them down on cards so you can repeat them during the day. You don't have to get down on your knees. All you have to do is create a quiet space in your mind. Speak the affirmations aloud, and create the life that you want. Do it daily. You'll be completely amazed at how they work.

****

All good things are available to me as a child of the Universe. As a parent provides and supplies all the essentials of life to a child, so the Great Spirit provides me with the power to create all good things. My life is mine to mold into an image of greatness. Complete faith is my constant companion.

Great and powerful Spirit who guides and inspires me, thank you for helping me to enjoy the blessings of this life. I am filled with gratitude—I have the eyes to see and the ears to hear the majesty that surrounds me. I affirm my ability to perceive the magnificence of this life.

I have counted on Spirit as my ally, and I have won my battles. I realize that my principle battle has been with myself—keeping myself away from all good things that are available to me in great abundance. I affirm that I am receiving all the good that is due me as I move forward with a light heart and joyous outlook.

I give thanks for my expanded awareness. I understand the complexity of this fabulous world and I marvel at the wonders that are before me. I daily see the gifts of God with new eyes, and am thankful for the blessings that rain down on me.

Joy is my constant companion, satisfaction and peace the goals that I have attained. My spirit reaches for the sky and rejoices as it touches all that is good. Heaven is my partner, earth is my teacher, and I continuously grow in power and love.

I have achieved a state of grace. I ask my angels to guide me so that I may always have peace in my soul. As I learn the lessons of this earth, I move happily and with lightness of step, for I know that Spirit is always by my side.

Fear is a myth; fear is a paper tiger. I am more than equal to this situation and I ask Spirit to be by my side as I vanquish negative feelings and face the light. Light always casts out darkness, and the light of Spirit will cast out all fear. I am victorious.

Health, happiness and joy belong to me by birthright, and my life is a shining example of these achievements. Others are inspired by the light I possess, and I realize that my contentedness comes from God. All things are channeled to me via Spirit. I am blessed.

Affirmations for Positive Fulfillment

My awareness is expanded—I am free to see the blessings that rain down upon me. I truly learn the lessons in this life so that difficulty is avoided and happiness becomes the order of the day. I have achieved my goal of contentment.

Intuition is my guide, my compass, and my shining star. I rely on the God-Spirit within to paint the way toward all good things. I have the ability to shun the negative talk of others and follow my true path. Success and contentment are my rewards.

With Spirit at my side I march fearlessly to the tune of my own drummer. As a result, my days are filled with wonder and difficulties are deflected and avoided. I rest easily each evening with dreams of my perfect life.

I see and appreciate the good that surrounds me. I fend off unpleasantness with the radiance of my light, and I allow Spirit to transcend all wickedness and fill my heart with gladness. I am thankful for the beauty that reveals itself to me in this life.

My goals are achieved with the help of Spirit. I have prepared the way for my success, and now I realize that it is my partnership with the essence of the universe that creates magic. My dreams and desires are realized as I speak.

Any difficulties I may have with another are simply an outward manifestation of a lesson I must learn. I walk with God and am *shown the paths to peaceful coexistence with others. A new and delightful relationship ensues as I let anxiety fall away and replace it with acceptance.*

Love is everywhere in my life, therefore I manifest the perfect life partner. My energy attracts those who share my outlook. Since like attracts like, I am unalterably attracted to my mate and best friend. I affirm the happiness and perfection of my relationship to those with whom I share my life.

My life is a shining beacon to others, that they may know the incandescence of Spirit. Through my attitude and works I hold myself to the highest standard of light, and continually strive to improve the world by my own example.

From my heart-space I send out the light of the universe to all people so that pain and suffering may diminish. I bathe the earth in love, and my light combined with the light of others creates a healing balm that cannot be denied. The Earth Mother and all her people receive the benefits of that magic.

The kingdom of Heaven is at hand

THE BOOK OF MATTHEW

13

Treasures from Edna's Kitchen

*M*om (to Edna): *"You shouldn't give Mandy choco-late—it's not good for her!"*

Edna: "Carol, chocolate is God's way of saying he loves us. They don't tell you this is in the Bible, but actually, on the seventh day, God did one last thing be-fore he rested. He made chocolate. Then, and only then, was he done."

That's my grandmother, irreverent as ever.

I'm lucky enough to have some recipes that were Edna's. She left me a treasure trove of herbal remedies that form one of the cornerstones for my own healing work.

She also left me recipes for her Chocolate-Coconut Cake (capitalized because it was famous within our family) and other special occasion sweets. She also left instructions for "elf and fairy food."

There were special delights like violet syrup and rose jam—sweet lovelies made from her precious flowers. I offer you these treasures in the same spirit as she made them—with joy and the anticipation of a visit from an angel!

I also decided to add her recipe for "Gorgeous Water," a homemade preparation for her facial skin that she used all the time. She had lovely skin—give it a try!

Herbal Teas

These are teas that Edna made with either fresh or dried herbs when we were feeling "under the weather." She would mix equal parts of the herbs in a tea strainer, pour hot water over them, and steep for about 2 minutes. Feel free to add a touch of honey if you like.

Tummy Trouble (Indigestion) Tea: **Sage, Anise, and Caraway**

"Dull Company" (Sleepy) Tea: **Catnip, Valerian, Clove**

Snuffle (Cold and Flu) Tea: **Eucalyptus, Mullein, Irish Moss, Slippery Elm, Spearmint**

(By the way, Edna had sources to buy dried herbs that were not available locally. In her day, it was mostly word of mouth. Today, these herbs are available in most large health food stores and some specialty markets.)

Violet Syrup

This is an excellent cough syrup, and something that Edna gave me whenever I felt under the weather. It has tonic-like effects, which basically means it just plain makes you feel better!

Take a quart mason jar and fill it with violet blossoms. Make sure that you have only flower petals, no stems or any green at all. Pour boiling water over the petals, and let it stand for a full day and night. Strain and discard the petals. You should have around a cup and a half of liquid. To the water add a tablespoon of lemon juice and 3 cups of sugar. Bring to a boil on top of the stove, and pour into small sterilized jars. Cap tightly and seal. I keep mine in the fridge where it will keep up to a month. Use it directly by the spoonful, or put a teaspoon in a cup of lovely mint tea.

Rose Jam
Eating roses on my toast makes me feel like a princess.

First of all, make sure that the roses you are using are completely free of pesticides. You'll need one firmly packed cup of prepared petals. To prepare, cut off the white part at the bottom —it's bitter. Edna used to put them in a bowl and mash them, but thanks to modern conveniences we can use a blender. Put the petals, juice of one lemon, ½ cup of water, and ¼ cup ginger ale in the blender and blend until smooth. Slowly add 2½ cups pectin according to instructions on box. Pour immediately into properly prepared jars and seal. It keeps for a few weeks in the fridge, and longer in the freezer.

Horehound and Catnip Cough Drops
Not only for coughs! Use when your throat is dry or sore, too.

By the way, you'll need a candy thermometer for this recipe.

Put ¼ cup each of Catnip and Horehound in a saucepan with 2 cups of water. Bring to boil, and let steep for about 15 minutes or so. Strain. Measure out a cup of this infusion and put to the side. In another bowl, add ⅛ teaspoon of cream of tartar to 2 cups of sugar. Sift them together. If you don't do this, the cream of tartar will lump up and it will be a mess. Pour the reserved infusion into a saucepan and add the dry mixture. Stir until sugar is dissolved, and cook over low heat. When the temperature hits 290 degrees on the candy thermometer, pour the mixture out onto a buttered plate or cutting board. When it's hardened slightly, score it into small squares. When almost hard, break the candy into pieces. Roll in corn starch. Store in a moisture-proof container.

Amber-Mint Jelly
My grandfather adored this.

Peel one grapefruit, one lemon, and one orange. Grind the fruit and measure. Cover with three times as much cold water as pulp and set aside until the next day.

Day two, boil it for 10 minutes. Set it aside until the next day! Day three, measure what you've got, and add an equal amount of sugar. Add 1 teaspoon of mint leaves. Boil until it jells. Put in sterile jars and refrigerate. Will keep for a couple of weeks.

Divinity

Edna never called this Divinity, it was always "Elf & Fairy Food." It's an old, old recipe written in an old-fashioned style, so be sure to read it through before trying it!

Put 2 cups sugar, ½ cup light corn syrup, and ½ cup cold water into a saucepan or iron skillet and cook over low heat, stirring just until sugar dissolves. Continue to cook without stirring until soft ball forms in water or mixture forms a thread when held up. While this mixture is cooking, beat 2 egg whites until stiff. When sugar mixture is ready, take it from heat and pour it slowly into egg whites, beating constantly. Add ⅛ tsp of vanilla. Beat mixture until it holds its shape. Add 1 cup of crushed walnuts and ½ cup loosely packed violet petals. Drop by teaspoonfuls on waxed paper. Allow to cool completely.

The Famous Chocolate-Coconut Cake

This cake would disappear within the space of 24 hours. Edna would blame it on the fairies, but I know it was my father and my grandfather who were the culprits.

Sift together the following:
>   2 cups cake flour
>   2¾ teaspoons baking powder
>   pinch of salt and pepper
>   1 ½ cups sugar

After you do that melt three squares of baking chocolate over low heat. In yet another bowl (a large one), cream together ⅔ cup shortening and 3 eggs. To that mixture add ¾ cup of milk and 1 teaspoon of vanilla. Then add the chocolate, beating constantly. Add the dry mixture and stir until just blended. Pour into greased and floured 8 inch cake pans and bake at 350 degrees for about 20-25 minutes (check using the toothpick test). Frost when completely cool with Edna's Chocolate Frosting.

Edna's Chocolate Frosting
In a word, yum.

Beat one cup softened butter, 1 pound confectioners sugar, 1 egg, 3 squares melted and slightly cooled baking chocolate, and 1 teaspoon vanilla until smooth and fluffy. After you frost the cake, decorate it with so much coconut that it actually looks furry. (For those of you who don't like coconut, you can leave out the last part…)

Gorgeous Water
Edna was blessed with soft, clear skin and few wrinkles. This lotion was a beauty staple. (PS: Don't drink this one—apply it topically! Use cotton balls or a mister)

Mix together ¼ cup each of Calendula and Rose petals. Put 2 cups of water in a saucepan. Add the flowers and the juice of one orange. Heat until just boiling. Cool completely, and then bottle the mixture. Will keep for a couple of weeks if refrigerated. Use morning and night before your moisturizer. Your skin will feel softer and smoother.

Be ye transformed by the renewing of your mind

THE BOOK OF ROMANS

14

Afterthought

*A*fter Edna died, I tried to continue my education in nature and her gifts. Mom and Dad thought that my experiments with herbs and flowers were just play, however, the equivalent of making sand castles. Without the support of Edna, I slowly stopped my communion with nature.

I had no more teachers at the time. I got involved with other things. I grew up into a nonconformist who confounded my parents and amused my friends. I had a variety of jobs, did a lot of theater, and went to California where I enjoyed small success as an actress. By small, I mean I managed to get enough work to join the Screen Actors Guild, but it looked like I was about to get a Masters degree in waiting tables. I always had a little apothecary shop in my kitchen, though. I made herbal remedies for myself and others—even their pets! It seemed like a hobby to me, a link with my long-deceased grandmother.

It wasn't until I went to a mystic in San Francisco that I realized what my path was in this life. This is what came through from Edna:

> *"I could make anyone feel better. If someone needed me, or needed my tinctures and flower cures, they knew where to find me. This wisdom and talent is a gift that*

*flows through the women in our family, and one that I
lovingly pass on to you..."*

After my tears, I realized that after all those years of searching for my calling, I had never looked in the obvious place. My own childhood.

Finding my way to this place in life has been a long road, and at times I've been tempted to give up. When life seemed too weird for words, I hung in there. Sometimes it truly is darkest before the dawn. The dawn came when I found the truth that was buried inside, and it came from the part of me that was still nine years old. Fancy that!

The darkness comes when we are blinded to the elements of God that are within us. Maeterlinck says, "What is man but a God who is afraid?"

Find that part of God that rests in your heart. Power does not exist in the past or the future—only in the now. Be joyful and fearless. Create a new world!

To learn, and from time to time apply what one has learned—isn't that a pleasure?

CONFUCIUS

Amanda Larson is a writer, spiritual coach and consultant in Washington, DC. She can be contacted at the following address:

The Larson Institute
PO Box 21241
Kalorama Station
Washington, DC 20009

Electronically she can be reached via her website:
www.larsoninstitute.org

DATE DUE